LIVING AND WORKING IN
ANCIENT CHINA

Edited by
Joanne Randolph

Enslow Publishing

101 W. 23rd Street
Suite 240
New York, NY 10011
USA

enslow.com

This edition published in 2018 by:
Enslow Publishing, LLC.
101 W. 23rd Street, Suite 240
New York, NY 10011

Library of Congress Cataloging-in-Publication Date

Names: Randolph, Joanne, editor.
Title: Living and working in ancient China / edited by Joanne Randolph.
Description: New York, NY : Enslow Publishing, 2018. | Series: Back in time | Includes bibliographical references and index.
Identifiers: LCCN 2017001861 | ISBN 9780766089631 (library bound book) | ISBN 9780766089617 (pbk. book) | ISBN 9780766089624 (6 pack)
Subjects: LCSH: China—Civilization—221 B.C.-960 A.D.—Juvenile literature. | China—Social life and customs—221 B.C.-960 A.D.—Juvenile literature.
Classification: LCC DS747.42 .L585 2018 | DDC 931—dc23
LC record available at https://lccn.loc.gov/2017001861

Printed in China

To Our Readers: We have done our best to make sure all website addresses in this book were active and appropriate when we went to press. However, the author and the publisher have no control over and assume no liability for the material available on those websites or on any websites they may link to. Any comments or suggestions can be sent by e-mail to customerservice@enslow.com.

Photos Credits: Cover, pp. 1 Liushengfilm/Shutterstock.com; series logo, jeedlove/Shutterstock.com; back cover, Reinhold Leitner/Shutterstock.com; hourglass on spine, MilaLiu/Shutterstock.com; pp. 4, 6, 17, 34 snvv/Shutterstock.com; p. 5 Private Collection/Ken Welsh/Bridgeman Images; p. 7 Florilegius/SSPL/Getty Images; p. 8 British Museum, London, UK/Bridgeman Images; p. 10 Stefano Bianchetti/Corbis Historical/Getty Images; p. 11 Print Collector/Hulton Archive/Getty Images; p. 13 Universal Images Group/Getty Images; p. 14 yanan mao/Moment/Getty Images; pp. 16, 20-21 Hulton Archive/Getty Images; pp. 18-19 Bibliotheque Municipale, Poitiers, France/Bridgeman Images; p. 22 Heritage Images/Hulton Archive/Getty Images; p. 25 Victoria & Albert Museum, London, UK/Bridgeman Images; pp. 27, 29 Science & Society Picture Library/Getty Images; p. 28 British Library, London, UK/© British Library Board. All Rights Reserved/Bridgeman Images; p. 31 Culture Club/Hulton Archives/Getty Images; pp. 32-33 adocphotos/Corbis Historical/Getty Images; p. 35 Visual China Group/Getty Images; p. 36 Pictures from History/Bridgeman Images; p. 37 Rischgitz/Hulton Archive/Getty Images.

Article Credits: Kathiann M. Kowalski, "Working on the Farm," *AppleSeeds*; Donna Henes, "While Adults Were Working," *AppleSeeds*; Kathiann M. Kowalski, "Who's in Charge?" *AppleSeeds*; Lori Soard, "The Golden Lotus: The Story of Tiny Feet," *AppleSeeds*; Christine Graf, "The Story of Silk," *AppleSeeds*; Louise L. Green, "Go Fly a Fengzheng!" *AppleSeeds*; Damian Fagan, "What to Do with Bamboo," *AppleSeeds*; Elizabeth Phillips-Hershey, "Engineering Water," *AppleSeeds*; Rochelle LeMaster, "How Can Water Tell Time?" *AppleSeeds*; Leigh Anderson, "The Fab 4: Chinese Inventions That Rocked the World," *AppleSeeds*; Kathiann M. Kowalski, "Word Pictures," *AppleSeeds*; Rochelle LeMaster, "The Gliding Horse," *AppleSeeds*; Donald Johnson, "Confucius: China's Great Teacher," *AppleSeeds*.

All articles © by Carus Publishing Company. Reproduced with permission.

All Cricket Media material is copyrighted by Carus Publishing Company, d/b/a Cricket Media, and/or various authors and illustrators. Any commercial use or distribution of material without permission is strictly prohibited. Please visit http://www.cricketmedia.com/info/licensing2 for licensing and http://www.cricketmedia.com for subscriptions.

CONTENTS

CHAPTER 1

ONE OF THE OLDEST CIVILIZATIONS

China is considered one of the oldest civilizations in the world. People have lived there for millions of years, and people began coming together to form communities along the Yellow and Yangtze Rivers thousands of years ago. China was ruled by an emperor in 2696 BCE, and soon dynasties formed. A dynasty is long line of hereditary rulers. Sometimes more than one dynasty or ruler wanted to control China. This meant there was often fighting.

Fighting was not the only thing happening in ancient China, though. The Chinese were working, creating art, and even inventing new things, such as the crossbow, silk, and paper. People worked to

This map shows China during the Hsia dynasty. It shows the distribution of people at around 2205 BCE.

build cities to house China's growing population, too. Even two thousand years ago, there were about sixty million people living in China. Today it has nearly 1.4 billion people living there, making it the most populous country in the world. Are you ready to find out more about life in ancient China?

CHAPTER 2

DAILY LIFE

The rich and the poor of ancient China led very different lives. Poor farmers worked hard to feed the country and their own families. And the children had to help their families in their homes and on the farms. The wealthy men who did not have to toil in the fields took positions in government, and rich girls suffered through the painful custom of foot binding for beauty.

WORKING ON THE FARM

With millions of mouths to feed, ancient China needed lots of food. No wonder most of its people were farmers.

Wheat, millet, and barley were the main crops in northern China. Southern China was warmer and wetter, so most farmers grew rice. Other crops included beans, squash, peas, berries, and melons. Farmers also grew hemp for making cloth. They raised chickens, ducks, sheep, pigs, and other animals.

Animals helped with some work. Several families in a village often shared an ox or water buffalo. In spring, the animals—and sometimes the people themselves—pulled plows that broke up soil before planting. At harvest time, they helped move crops and thresh grain.

Lots of farm work was done by hand or with simple tools. Watering and weeding crops had to be done constantly. Farmers also struggled to keep insects, birds, and other pests away.

Even when they used simple machines, people usually provided the power to run them. For example, the chain pump (invented around 100 BCE) was made of wooden paddles on a long chain. It was used

A water buffalo is shown dragging a harrow, which was a tool used to break up clumps of soil and smooth out the earth after plowing.

to pump water into fields instead of people having to carry the water from a river. To work the pump, people had to walk on a wheel at the top of the chain.

During busy times, such as the harvest seasons, everyone helped in the fields. But most of the time, men grew the crops, and boys helped as soon as they were old enough. Women and girls made clothes and shoes, prepared family meals, and gathered herbs for medicines. Many peasant women raised silkworms, too.

This watercolor illustration shows Chinese men operating the chain pump to water a rice field.

Farmers never knew how big their harvest would be. Bad weather or bugs could easily ruin crops. Plus, part of each year's crops had to be given to the government as taxes—even when families had very little.

At least one month each year, most peasant farmers also had to work for the government. They built palaces and royal tombs, dug irrigation ditches, and worked on pathways.

In ancient China, being a peasant farmer was an honorable job, but it was hard work!

RICE—THE NUMBER ONE CROP

Chinese people have grown rice for more than seven thousand years. By the time of the Han dynasty (206 BCE–220 CE), rice was the main food in much of southern China.

The Chinese grew rice in fields called paddies. Rice needs lots of clean water, so farmers built low dams to keep paddies flooded. Farmers controlled water levels in the paddies by letting water flow in and out through ditches.

Preparing paddies was easiest in low, flat areas. As farmers needed more land, they learned to build paddies on terraces. Terraces are like giant steps carved into hillsides. Farmers pumped water uphill from nearby rivers or ditches.

To grow rice, farmers started by soaking the seeds. After a day or two, they planted the seeds in wet, flooded soil. Three or four weeks later, they transplanted, or moved, the seedlings to bigger paddies. Bending over, the farmers thrust each tiny plant into the muddy soil.

Farmers kept the paddies wet while the plants grew larger. They also pulled weeds and did their best to keep their crops free of pests

Here, farmers are transplanting rice plants in a flooded rice paddy. Flooding the fields helps keep weeds down and pests away from the rice plants.

and diseases. Sometimes, farmers put oil on rice plants to kill bugs; other times, they pulled off the bugs with bamboo combs.

After three to six months, the rice was ready for harvest. Farmers let the water flow out, draining the paddies. Then they cut the rice stalks.

The next step was threshing to separate the rice kernels from the strawlike stalks. Sometimes, oxen helped by trampling on the straw. Farmers then collected the kernels from the threshing floor. Without oxen, farmers rocked back and forth on large "tilt hammers." The hammers crushed the grains underneath them.

After threshing, farmers picked out stones, sticks, and leaves. Last, the rice was milled to remove the hard outer hull. And finally, farmers' wives cooked the rice for family meals. Of course, some of the harvest was used to pay taxes, rent, and any other debts the farmer owed.

Rice farming methods have advanced since ancient times. Techniques vary in different parts of the world, too. But most Chinese rice farmers still have a hard job.

WHILE THE ADULTS WERE WORKING

For a long time in ancient China, children didn't go to school. They worked alongside their parents. Girls helped their mothers cook, clean, make clothing, and tend silkworms. Boys were more likely to work with their fathers outdoors, planting and harvesting crops. Then, more than two thousand years ago, Han emperor Wudi believed that education was the key to good government. He started a system of free schools for boys. Girls still worked and learned at home.

The top illustration shows the foot-operated mortar and pestle that pounded the tough rice grains. The middle image shows a seed drill used to plant seeds, and the bottom image shows the Chinese plow.

Chinese children still found time to play. They played board games such as backgammon and a game called Go. (Go was invented in China around 2000 BCE.) By 400 BCE, Xianqi, or Chinese chess, became popular. (In case you were wondering, Chinese checkers is not a Chinese game. It was invented in Germany.)

As in many places, rich and poor children had different toys and games. While they all played with balls, only wealthy children played polo, a ball game played on horseback. There was also a ball game similar to football.

Boys learned martial arts, archery, and hunting with trained falcons. Children in wealthier families played with silk-and-bamboo kites and ivory yo-yos with satin cords. And like people everywhere, all Chinese children enjoyed music, dancing, and festivals.

WHO'S IN CHARGE?

Today, China is a huge nation. More than two thousand years ago, China was already huge. For a long time, there was fighting among the provinces. Amazingly, Emperor Qin Shi Huangdi had stopped the fighting. But he couldn't run this new country all alone. So the emperor divided China into thirty-six districts. He named head officials to run the districts. Other people worked under those men.

This was the start of the civil service system in ancient China. Civil servants do a government's daily work. In ancient China, they enforced laws, collected taxes, and kept government records. They also ran building projects and provided protection from crime. In short, they ran the government.

嬴名政始自始皇乙卯即王位庚辰併天下稱皇帝

位三十七年居位二十五年即帝位十二年壽五十

Emperor Qin Shi Huangdi was emperor during China's Warring States period. In addition to starting the civil service system, he created a national road system.

"Exceptional work demands exceptional men," declared Emperor Wudi, ruler of the Han dynasty from 140 BCE to 87 BCE. Wudi wanted only the best people in government. He told district officials to "search for men of brilliant and exceptional talents."

Of course, anyone who worked for the government needed to be trained, so Emperor Wudi started a National Academy. Graduates had to pass a final exam to get a civil service job. In the beginning, job candidates answered test questions orally. (That is, they spoke the answers rather than writing them down.) The questions were about laws and other topics, and they weren't too difficult. Later on, tests included written questions and answers.

Over time, the exams became harder and covered more subjects. During the T'ang dynasty, for example, civil service tests asked questions about literature, philosophy, and other difficult subjects.

Many men wanted civil service jobs, and competition was tough. Those who scored the highest on the tests got the best jobs. Low scorers might not get any job at all.

Not all people in ancient China could join the civil service. For example, most farmers did not go to school, so

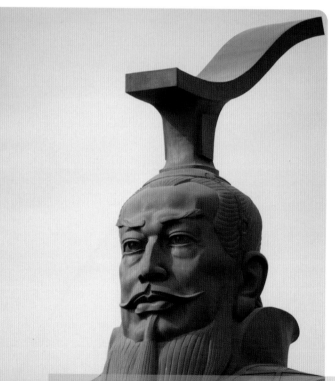

Wudi was the seventh emperor of the Han dynasty. He was known as a great leader.

they could not take the tests and pass. Women were not allowed to hold civil service jobs.

It might seem that some people had an unfair advantage over others in the civil service tests, but these tests were important. The goal was to give the best government jobs to the best people.

Modern China has its own civil service system. After all, governments still have lots of work to do. And they want smart people to do those jobs.

THE GOLDEN LOTUS: THE STORY OF TINY FEET

How do people today change their bodies? What do we do to make ourselves seem more beautiful or more like celebrities? For women in long ago China, it was all about feet!

They say it began about one thousand years ago. Tiny feet were considered beautiful. The "perfect" woman's foot was called the "Golden Lotus" and was only 3 or 4 inches (8 to 10 centimeters) long! To create Golden Lotus feet, a mother began to bind her little daughter's feet tightly with cloth bandages.

First, the girl's feet were soaked in hot water and rubbed to soften them so they could be bent. Next, the mother bent her daughter's four smallest toes and arch under, then wrapped bandages tightly around each foot, to hold it in this bent position. Every day, the mother rewrapped the bandages, more tightly and very painfully each time. Some girls died of infections that began in their feet.

This process went on for several years. During that time, many of the bones in the girl's feet broke. By the end she could

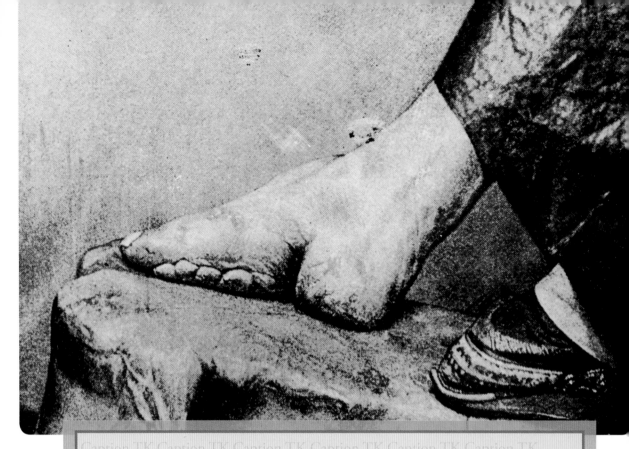

Women's feet were horribly deformed by foot binding. This image shows the lotus feet of a wealthy Chinese woman.

hardly walk, and certainly could not run, dance, or do any work that required standing for a long time.

Why would a woman do this to her daughter? A future husband thought a girl with Golden Lotus feet would be more obedient. After all, she could hardly walk. Bound feet were also a status symbol. They showed that a woman did not have to work in the fields, as farmers did. By the 1930s, the practice was illegal and had finally stopped.

CHAPTER 3

ANCIENT CHINESE INVENTIONS

S everal ancient Chinese innovations changed the course of human history. We continue to use these fabulous inventions today. Can you guess what they are? One is explosive, one is a traveler's aid, one is used to make clothing, one is fun on a windy day, one tells time, and the other two help us communicate and record our ideas.

THE STORY OF SILK

Si-Ling-Chi was the empress of China around 2700 BCE. Legend tells us that she discovered silk after noticing a silkworm cocoon in a mulberry tree. Many Chinese families became silk farmers following her discovery.

Unlike most farmers, silk farmers don't plant crops or tend fields. Instead, they take care of silkworms that hatch out of their eggs in the spring. Before they hatched, silk farmers carried them in special belts next to their bodies to keep them warm.

Once the eggs hatched, they placed the tiny black silkworms in flat trays inside their homes. The tiny worms have huge appetites—they can eat fifty times their weight in mulberry leaves! They make so much noise when they are munching on their leaves that it sounds like falling rain.

Keeping the hungry worms fed took a lot of work because they need to eat eight times a day. The women and girls gathered the tender leaves from mulberry trees. They chopped them into tiny pieces for the worms. They also cleaned their trays every day to keep them dry and free from ants. If ants got into the trays, they would eat the precious silkworms. That would not be a good thing!

For about thirty to forty days, the worms would eat and eat. Then they would be ready to build cocoons on twigs that the farmers placed in their trays. The worms spent three or four days wrapping their bodies in the silk that comes out of two openings under their mouths. The slightest noise could cause them to stop spinning. So, the farmers had to be very quiet around them.

After three or four days, silk farmers carefully removed the cocoons from the twigs, placed them into baskets, and took them to the market to sell. Whoever bought the cocoons had to place them into hot water. This killed the pupae before they became moths and broke out of the cocoons. (The pupae are the life form between a worm and a moth.) This is important. If a moth came out, it would cut through its cocoon, breaking the silk thread. This would have ruined the silk thread. The silk that was unwound from the

Chinese women wove the silk threads into cloth using a loom, such as the one shown here.

cocoons was delicate. Many strands had to be twisted together to make strong silk thread. The girls and women who did this job in ancient China had to be good with their hands. They also needed to be patient because it takes three thousand cocoons to make a pound (about half a kilogram) of silk (two thousand cocoons make one dress). The silk thread was then sent to women who wove the thread into beautiful cloth. Silk was important to ancient China. At that

Chinese people have been flying kites on the Double Ninth Festival since ancient times. Do you see the bird and dragon kites shown in this engraving of people celebrating this holiday?

time, people in other countries did not know how to make silk, so they had to buy it from China. It was so valuable that the Chinese emperor decreed that anyone who was caught sharing silk-making secrets or sneaking silkworms out of the country would be killed.

GO FLY A FENGZHENG!

Have you ever flown a kite on a windy day? The Chinese word for kite is *fengzheng*. *Feng* (it rhymes with "hung") means "wind." *Zheng* (it sounds like "jung") means "compete." This is because a fengzheng is in a contest with the wind as it tosses, dips, and glides in the sky.

China is the homeland of the kite. For more than two thousand years, the Chinese have built kites, at first out of bamboo and silk. According to tradition, they created kites to try to fly to heaven.

Later, the Chinese used kites as tools to set fishing lines far from a boat, to carry messages, and to measure distance. Legend says they used kite noises to frighten enemies. Sound was added by fixing whistles and pipes to the kite line for the wind to blow through. Enemies thought they were hearing the voices of gods.

Because of their kite designs, the Chinese learned about air currents, balance, wind changes, and gliding a long time before the rest of the world did. The great Italian traveler Marco Polo wrote about men gliding in kites in China more than seven hundred years ago.

So, the next time you fly a fengzheng, remember that you are experiencing part of Chinese history as you compete with the wind.

WHAT TO DO WITH BAMBOO

Bamboo was an important plant in the lives of the ancient Chinese. Many household items—even the houses themselves—were made from the strong stems of this fast-growing grass. (Yes, bamboo is a member of the grass family.) Craftspeople made tables, baskets, mats, bowls, ladders, fish traps, rakes, rafts, and chopsticks from bamboo. Young plants were harvested for food.

Bamboo grew (and still grows today) throughout much of southern China. There are many different types of bamboo. Some have thin stems and grow to only 10 feet (3 meters) tall. Other kinds are 7 inches (18 cm) in diameter and can be 100 feet (30.5 m) tall! The hard, woody stems are mostly hollow and look like straws taped together end to end.

This bamboo carving shows a scholar leaning on a rock. The base of the carving is made from boxwood, not bamboo.

In ancient China, bamboo was harvested in the late fall. It took several chops from a hatchet to cut through the stems. Then the shoots could be used in many ways. Before the Chinese invented paper, they made books out of thin strips of bamboo. As you might imagine, these books were clumsy to handle and took up a lot of space. It would have been hard to read a book if one of the strips was lost! Then, in the year 105, a Chinese man made the first paper. Guess what one of the ingredients was? That's right—bamboo!

Writing was not the only art form to use bamboo. Music in ancient China would not have been the same without this amazing plant. Craftspeople made eighteen flutes and pipes from a hollow stem. Once a section of bamboo was cut to length, small holes were drilled into the tube. This allowed the musician to play different notes. One type of instrument was made of several pieces of bamboo cut to different lengths. This Sheng, or "mouth organ," was like a cross between a harmonica and a flute. The musician blew or sucked air while using one or more fingers to cover the pipes' holes.

Many children's toys, such as dolls, kites, stilts, and whistles, were made of bamboo. One toy, the bamboo dragonfly, was a small propeller attached to a stick that rose into the air when spun between two hands. In ancient China, people watched tall bamboo trees swaying in strong winds, and they saw that this tree would bend but not break. So, in addition to being a useful material, bamboo became a symbol of strength and flexibility during difficult times.

Many years later, a Chinese toy dragonfly inspired Britain's Sir George Cayley (1796–1855) to study the concept of flight. Cayley later became the "Father of Aviation."

ENGINEERING WATER

In ancient China, people believed that a magical "Emperor Yu" held the secret for taming the rivers that flooded each season. The myth said that he was given mathematical secrets by a river tortoise. The secrets told him how to build canals, dikes, and irrigation systems. But it was real-life engineers and laborers—men and women, children and the elderly—who were responsible for the actual building.

Early Chinese civilizations were built on the low plains along the Yellow and Yangtze Rivers. These rivers, and the smaller rivers that fed them, were both helpful and destructive. They provided water for growing crops and were a means of transportation. Often, though, floods destroyed the fields. To prevent water from destroying crops, workers built earthen walls. They dug more channels into which floodwater could go.

In the hills of northern China, crops were grown on terraces cut into hillsides. People invented irrigation machines so they wouldn't have to carry water by hand. One such invention was like a stationary bicycle: two people pedaled to bring water from wells, reservoirs, and canals through a wooden channel and into a raised ditch.

As populations grew and new cities were built, Chinese engineers designed a network of canals to connect the country. The emperors supported these efforts which helped speed the movement of military troops and supplies and expanded trade.

One of the most amazing feats of water engineering in ancient China was the construction of the Grand Canal. Some parts of this waterway were built almost twenty-five hundred years ago. It was finished around the year 600. The canal is more than 1,100 miles

(1,770 kilometers) long. (That's about the same distance as from New York to Florida.) About sixty bridges cross it. Like other canals, the Grand Canal was used for trade and transportation.

But these canals, like other great structures, were built under difficult conditions: Millions of workers were forced to work on the canals. In some areas of China, every male from the age of fifteen to fifty-five had to join the work forces. Women became laborers for the first time in the year 608 to work on the Grand Canal. Children and the elderly helped. Nearly two million people died building the Grand Canal. Like natural rivers that flow and flood, engineering water was both helpful and destructive to the people of ancient China.

The Grand Canal is the longest canal in the world. It is also one of the oldest canals.

How Can Water Tell Time?

In 1090, Su-Song was ordered by the emperor to build a clock tower for the capital city. Others before him had used water for time telling, but Su-Song's clock was more complex and more accurate than the others. To create power, Su-Song constructed a 40-foot-tall (12-meter-tall) tower. Inside the tower was a large bucket-lined water wheel. Water flowed steadily over it. As each bucket on the wheel filled with water, it fell forward, pulling the empty bucket behind it under the spout. The movement set off bells, gongs, or drums every fifteen minutes. These announced the correct time to all who heard them.

Gunpowder

Many ancient Chinese alchemists wanted to invent a potion that could make people live forever. Somewhere between 150 and 850, an alchemist cooked up a black powdery mixture. It didn't make people live forever. Instead, it exploded! The Chinese called this mixture *huo yao*, or "fire chemical." Soon after, they began stuffing huo yao into bamboo pipes and paper tubes to make firecrackers to scare away evil spirits. Later, alchemists added more of a chemical called saltpeter to the mixture. Bang! Huo yao became the gunpowder we know today.

By the year 1000, the Chinese were using gunpowder as a weapon. They shot at enemies with arrows armed with firecrackers. Later, the Chinese discovered that if they left the ends of the paper tubes open, the firecrackers would shoot wildly along the ground like rats. This scared the enemy and their horses. Some shot accidentally into the air! It wasn't long before the Chinese started working on rockets.

This is part of a model of the Chinese astronomical clock, showing the water wheel. There are thirty-six buckets in the water wheel.

The revolving wheel was a weapon the Chinese developed that used gunpowder. It could be carried by a horse and then placed on the ground to fire. It allowed multiple shots to be fired quickly.

THE COMPASS

Historians aren't sure exactly when the ancient Chinese invented the first compass. Somewhere between 770 and 221 BCE, Chinese miners realized that magnetic lodestone (iron ore) aligns itself along a north-south line. The first compasses weren't made for use by explorers, however. Spiritualists and fortune-tellers made and used them to predict the future. They also used compasses to help people

This is a wooden feng shui compass that was used to help position buildings in a lucky way.

build their houses or place objects along the "lucky" north-south line. (South was considered the lucky direction.)

Early compasses were called "south-pointers." They had spoon-shaped lodestones resting on square bronze plates with circular centers. The handle of the spoon always pointed south. Over time, south-pointers began to be used as direction finders. Eventually, the Chinese began using needles that had been rubbed on lodestones to magnetize them. These magnetized needles soon replaced the heavy spoon-shaped stones. This made compasses much easier to carry. By the year 1000, travelers and explorers were using compasses to find their way.

PAPER

The Chinese invented paper during the Han dynasty. That first paper was made from hemp plant fibers. It was heavy and spongy. The Chinese used it for clothing! They wrote on strips of silk or bamboo. Then, in the year 105, an imperial court officer named Cai Lun presented the emperor with a smoother, lighter-weight paper made from mulberry tree bark. A new industry was born.

Soon, Chinese papermakers were making paper from a mixture of bamboo fibers, tree bark, rags, old fishnets, hemp, and other plants. They boiled this mixture for over a month, then pounded the fibers and strained out the water, leaving a smooth, thin layer. These sheets dried into paper that was good to write on. "Cai Lun Paper" was easy to make, inexpensive, and popular. It made Cai Lun a rich man.

WORD PICTURES

Chinese handwriting dates back more than three thousand years and is written in characters. Characters began as pictograms, or word pictures. The ancient character for "water" resembled ripples of water. "Bird" was a stick figure bird. There are more than forty thousand characters in a Chinese dictionary. Most people need to know about three thousand to four thousand characters to read a newspaper.

After Emperor Qin united China in 221 BCE, people used just one writing style. Today, China's 1.2 billion people speak about three thousand dialects. Yet they use one written language.

Only rich boys learned to write in ancient China. Students memorized dozens of characters each week. They painted word pictures with brushes and ink.

Modern simplified Chinese writing uses thousands of characters. Many characters have changed from their ancient forms. Some characters combine radicals (basic characters). Still more characters add phonetics (sound symbols) to radicals.

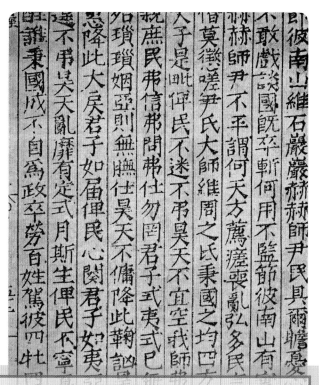

This page from the *I Ching*, or *Book of Changes*, shows lots of Chinese characters. The *I Ching* is a famous divination text. Diviners are people who try to answer questions or predict the future using different ritualized methods.

PRINTING

What if you had to write ten thousand copies of this book by hand? It would take you a long time! For hundreds of years, the Chinese printed pages of text from wood blocks. For each page of text, a separate block of wood was carved, inked, and printed on a sheet of paper. While faster than writing each page by hand, this process was time consuming. Then, in the year 1041, a man named Bi Sheng began using "movable type." Instead of carving one page of text on a block, he made individual characters from clay, allowed them to dry, and arranged the hardened pieces into text within a frame or press. After printing a page, Bi Sheng removed the pieces and reused them for other texts. These movable characters could be used over and over again.

Printing in Chinese was still hard work. Printers had to make and use thousands of clay pieces, because there are so many Chinese characters. (When Germany's Johannes Gutenberg created his printing press four hundred years later, he made pieces for only twenty-six alphabet letters.)

THE GLIDING HORSE

Sometime between 200 BCE and 200 CE, the great Chinese general Chuko Liang faced a difficult task. He needed to deliver supplies to his soldiers and remove wounded men from the battlefield. He is credited for inventing the wheelbarrow to solve his task. General Liang's wheelbarrow consisted of one wheel set between two long wooden boxes. Easily pushed, this wheelbarrow was known as the "gliding horse." For the heaviest loads, the wheelbarrow could be made with two wheels and pulled. The two-wheeled model, called the "wooden ox," required two men to lift it and steer.

Wheelbarrows made it easier for Chinese farmers to transport their goods to market, among many other different kinds of jobs.

CHAPTER 4

IMPORTANT PEOPLE IN ANCIENT CHINA

M any great people throughout China's long history worked hard to make the country what it is today. These influential individuals include Qin Shi Huangdi, who, as previously mentioned, ended the fighting between states; Liu Bang, a peasant who rose to the emperor's throne; and Confucius, the fifth-century BCE philosopher who continues to shape the way of thinking in China even in modern times.

QIN SHI HUANGDI

In 221 BCE, China was first unified under the Qin people. Their leader, born Ying Zheng, named himself Qin Shi Huangdi, meaning "First Emperor of Qin." He formed a strong centralized government and standardized weights and measures, money, and the writing system. He also had many palaces and lots of roads to link the provinces to the capital city. He also built an early version of the Great Wall of China in order to keep out raiding forces. He died in 210 BCE and the Qin dynasty was replaced by the Han dynasty a few years later.

This is part of the Great Wall built by Qin Shi Huangdi.

漢高祖 劉邦

Liu Bang was called Emperor Gao or Gaozu during his rule.

LIU BANG AND THE RISE OF THE HAN DYNASTY

The Han dynasty was originally founded by a rebel leader named Liu Bang. The Han dynasty lasted around four centuries and was considered the golden age of Chinese history. It was known for its economic prosperity and also for its many innovations, such as the ones we learned about in the last chapter. Liu Bang had risen from a poor background to be a leader in the Qin society. When Qin Shi Huangdi died, Liu Bang gave up his position and became a leader in the Qin opposition. He ruled from 202 to 195 BCE.

CONFUCIUS: CHINA'S GREAT TEACHER

Confucius (551-479 BCE) was China's great teacher. His ideas were the basis of China's civil service examinations. Chinese leaders looked to him to learn how to rule honestly.

Confucianism is a system of beliefs based on the teachings of Confucius. It is still followed by many people today.

Confucian teachings centered on the family. He believed that each child could become a good person by following the proper example of older family members. If children respected and obeyed their elders—especially their parents—he was sure there would be good families and in turn good government.

Confucius taught filial piety, which means respect and love for one's parents. He told children: "Behave in such a way that your parents only have to worry about your health." Be modest and don't talk too much, don't exaggerate or hog the conversation. If things go wrong, don't blame others; blame yourself and think what you can do to make things better.

Confucius spent his life teaching how to create a peaceful society. His ideas continue to inspire people in China even today.

c. 6500 BCE Rice cultivation begins in the Yangtze River valley in China.

c. 5000–3000 BCE Yangshao culture thrives in Yellow River valley, China.

5000 BCE Villages arise in China around the Yellow River. Terraced farming begins and rice is cultivated.

2070–1600 BCE Xia dynasty is the first dynasty recorded in ancient Chinese historical chronicles.

c. 1600–1046 BCE The Shang dynasty in China.

c. 1250 BCE Writing develops in China during the Shang dynasty.

1046–226 BCE The Zhou dynasty in China.

772–476 BCE The Spring and Autumn period.

771–226 BCE Eastern Zhou dynasty in China.

551–479 BCE Life of Confucius.

512–506 BCE The Wu Chu wars in China between the states of Wu and Chu.

476–221 BCE Warring States period in China.

328–308 BCE Rise of the Chinese state of Qin.

262–260 BCE The Battle of Changping, one of the most important battles in the Warring States period in China between Zhao and Qin.

259 BCE Qin Shi Huangdi, first emperor of China, is born.

256 BCE The army of the state of Qin captures the city of Chengzhou and the last Zhou ruler, King Nan, is killed, ending the Zhou dynasty.

c. 221 BCE Qin Shi Huangdi constructs the Northern Frontier wall, precursor to the Great Wall.

221–206 BCE Qin dynasty; Emperor Qin Shi Huangdi adopts legalism as state philosophy and bans all others.

210–206 BCE China rises in rebellion against the crumbling Qin dynasty.

210 BCE First emperor of China Qin Shi Huangdi dies and is buried with an army of eight thousand terra-cotta warriors in a palace tomb.

206 BCE–9 CE The Han dynasty rules China from their capital in Chang'an.

206–202 BCE The Chu–Han Contention divides China.

Liu-Bang of Han battles Xiang-Yu of Chu for supremacy of rule.

202 BCE Liu Bang is proclaimed emperor of China after defeating the rebel Xiang Yu.

202 BCE–220 CE The Han dynasty in China.

195 BCE Liu Bang dies. His empress Lü Zhi (also known as Lü Hou) tries to confiscate the empire for her own family. The conflict lasts for fifteen years.

141–87 BCE Reign of Emperor Wu (also known as Wudi).

138–126 BCE Zhang Qian, as envoy of the Han emperor, opens up the Silk Road trading route between China and central Asia.

129 BCE Parthians conquer Mesopotamia. The Silk Road to China is now controlled by the Parthians.

117–100 BCE Han emperors extend the western part of the Great Wall of China.

109 BCE Chinese Han Empire conquers the kingdom of Tien.

9 CE–23 CE Wang Man takes control of the empire by usurping the throne and proclaiming the beginning of a new dynasty called Xin, or "new."

25–220 CE The Eastern Han dynasty rules China.

91 CE The Han dynasty of China invades Mongolia.

160 CE Chinese Han empire in decline.

168–189 CE Ling is emperor in China.

190 CE Dong Zhou seizes control of the Chinese imperial capital and places a child, Liu Xie, as the new ruler.

208 CE China is divided into three regional kingdoms.

220 CE Liu Xie abdicates the throne. Wars between warlords and states continue, and China will have to wait about 350 years to be unified again.

304 CE The nomadic Xiongu break through the Great Wall of China.

589–618 CE Sui dynasty in China.

598–649 CE Life of Li-Shimin, Emperor Taizong of China.

618–626 CE Reign of Gaozu, first emperor of Tang dynasty in China.

618–907 CE The Tang dynasty in China.

624–705 CE Life of Wu Zhao, Empress Wu Zetian of China.

626–649 CE Reign of Emperor Taizong in China.

634 CE Taizong signs peace treaty between Tibet and China.

649–683 CE Reign of Emperor Gaozong in China.

683–704 CE Reign of Empress Wu Zetian, only female monarch of China.

685–762 CE Life of Li Longji, Emperor Xuanzong of China.

712–756 CE Reign of Xuanzong, seventh emperor of the Tang dynasty in China.

713–737 CE Golden Age of the reign of Xuanzong in China.

756–762 CE Reign of Emperor Suzong in China.

907 CE Zhu Wen establishes the Later Liang dynasty in China; the start of the Five Dynasties.

907–960 CE The Five Dynasties and Ten Kingdoms period in China.

960–1234 CE The Sung dynasty in China.

GLOSSARY

alchemist A person who studied a form of chemistry and philosophy that was focused on the transformation of matter, particularly turning base metals into gold.

civilization The society, culture, and way of life of a particular people in a certain area.

civil service The branches of government that deal with all governmental administrative functions outside of the military.

cocoon A silky case spun by the larval (baby) stage of many insects for protection in the pupal stage.

district A distinct area or neighborhood.

dynasty A line of hereditary rulers of a country.

engineering The branch of science and technology concerned with the design, building and use of engines, machines, and structures.

irrigation The manmade method by which water is supplied to plants grown for agricultural purposes.

lodestone A piece of magnetite or other naturally magnetic mineral able to be used as a magnet.

magnetic Something that is capable of being attracted by a magnet.

paddies Fields where rice is grown.

phonetics The sounds of a language when spoken.

province A principal administrative division or certain countries or empires.

pupae Insects in their inactive stage between the larvae and adult stages of development.

radical The root of a word or most basic unit of a character.

reservoir A place where a community's water supply is kept.

status symbol Something that shows a person's high place in society.

terrace A level, flat area cut into sloping land that resembles a step.

thresh To separate the seeds or grain from a plant.

transplant To move to another place.

FURTHER READING

BOOKS

Campbell, Trenton. *Gods and Goddesses of Ancient China*. New York, NY: Rosen Publishing, 2014.

Kovacs, Vic. *The Culture of the Qin and Han Dynasties of Ancient China*. New York, NY: PowerKids Press, 2016.

Leusted, Marcia Amidon. *Ancient Chinese Daily Life*. New York, NY: Rosen Young Adult, 2016.

Morrow, Paula. *Ancient Chinese Culture*. New York, NY: Rosen Young Adult, 2016.

Sonneborn, Liz. *Ancient China*. New York, NY: Children's Press, 2012.

Xu, Jay. *Tomb Treasures: New Discoveries from China's Han Dynasty*. San Francisco, CA: Asian Art Museum, 2017.

WEBSITES

The British Museum
www.ancientchina.co.uk/menu.html
Explore ancient Chinese history and culture through crafts,
geography, tombs, writing, and more.

DK Find Out!
www.dkfindout.com/us/history/ancient-china/
Learn more about the basic history of ancient China, including
information about the first emperor, inventions, and the
building of the Great Wall of China.

KidsKonnect
kidskonnect.com/history/ancient-china/
A quick reference to facts on ancient China.

INDEX